TERRIFIC TEAMS

Meet the DALLAS COWBOYS

PERCY LEED

Lerner Publications ◆ Minneapolis

Stats in this book are accurate through the 2023 National Football League season.

Lerner Publications Company
An imprint of Lerner Publishing Group, Inc.
241 First Avenue North
Minneapolis, MN 55401 USA

For reading levels and more information, look up this title at www.lernerbooks.com.

Main body text set in ITC Avant Garde Gothic Std.
Typeface provided by Adobe Systems.

Designer: Mary Ross **Photo Editor:** Lucien Brinkley

Library of Congress Cataloging-in-Publication Data

Names: Leed, Percy, 1968- author.
Title: Meet the Dallas Cowboys / Percy Leed.
Description: Minneapolis : Lerner Publications , [2026] | Series: Terrific teams (Lerner sports rookie) | Includes bibliographical references and index. | Audience: Ages 5–8 | Audience: Grades 2–3 | Summary: "The Dallas Cowboys are the most popular football team in the NFL. Explore the big-time superstars and iconic victories the Cowboys are known for, and find out why fans call them America's Team"— Provided by publisher.
Identifiers: LCCN 2024041501 (print) | LCCN 2024041502 (ebook) | ISBN 9798765668429 (library binding) | ISBN 9798765683651 (paperback) | ISBN 9798765681732 (epub)
Subjects: LCSH: Dallas Cowboys (Football team)—Juvenile literature.
Classification: LCC GV956.D3 L443 2026 (print) | LCC GV956.D3 (ebook) | DDC 796.332/64097642812—dc23/eng/20241009

LC record available at https://lccn.loc.gov/2024041501
LC ebook record available at https://lccn.loc.gov/2024041502

Manufactured in the United States of America
1-1011743-53810-10/30/2024

Photo Acknowledgments
Image credits: Ryan Kang/Getty Images, pp. 5, 11, 22; AP Photo/Matt Patterson, p. 7; AP Photo/Al Messerschmidt, p. 9; Peter Read Miller via AP, p. 13; Focus on Sport/Getty Images, p. 14; Eakin Howard/Getty Images, p. 16; Kevin Sabitus/Getty Images, p. 19; AP Photo/Sam Hodde, p. 20; Stacy Revere/Getty Images, p. 23. Design elements: Andrii Shelenkov/Getty Images; Kwangmoozaa/Getty Images.
Cover: Perry Knotts via AP.

Table of Contents

Dak Prescott threw the football.
CeeDee Lamb ran to catch it.
Touchdown!

The Dallas Cowboys started playing in the NFL in 1960.

The Cowboys play home games in Arlington, Texas. They have fans all around the United States.

Fans call the Cowboys America's Team.

Big Moments

The Cowboys have won the Super Bowl five times. Only two other teams have won more Super Bowls.

The Cowboys won their first Super Bowl in 1972. They beat the Miami Dolphins on a cold day.

Dallas won a close game against the San Francisco 49ers to reach the 1993 Super Bowl. Then the Cowboys crushed the Buffalo Bills 52–17.

In 2023, the Cowboys played the New York Giants in the season's first game. The Cowboys won 40–0.

Best Players

Bob Lilly's defense helped Dallas win the 1972 Super Bowl. His nickname is Mr. Cowboy.

Quarterback Roger Staubach led the Cowboys to four Super Bowls in the 1970s.

The Cowboys were great in the 1990s. Quarterback Troy Aikman helped the team win three Super Bowls.

Aikman played with running back Emmitt Smith. Smith is the NFL's all-time leader in rushing yards.

Micah Parsons is a strong defender. He had 14 sacks in 2023.

Quarterback Dak Prescott and wide receiver CeeDee Lamb are great players. Prescott threw 14 touchdown passes to Lamb in 2023.

★ CHAPTER 4 ★

Let's Go, Cowboys!

The Cowboys have a star on their helmets. It stands for the Texas nickname the Lone Star State.

The Cowboys always play on Thanksgiving Day.

Many fans love to eat and watch football with family on Thanksgiving Day.

The Cowboys last played in the Super Bowl in 1996. Fans can't wait for them to return to the big game!

DALLAS COWBOYS TEAM LEADERS

Passing touchdowns:	Tony Romo, 248
Passing yards:	Tony Romo, 34,183
Rushing yards:	Emmitt Smith, 17,162
Rushing touchdowns:	Emmitt Smith, 153
Tackles:	Darren Woodson, 827

Glossary

NFL: National Football League

sack: when a quarterback is tackled for a loss of yards

Super Bowl: the NFL's championship game

Learn More

Downs, Kieran. *Football*. Minneapolis: Bellwether Media, 2024.

Huddleston, Emma. *Get Ready for a Football Game*. Minneapolis: Bearport, 2024.

Leed, Percy. *Football's Super Bowl*. Minneapolis: Lerner Publications, 2025.

Index